Candi -
Start from within
you

Become You

A Transformational Blueprint for your Mind, Body, and Soul

Toneka R. Etienne, PhD

For media or print interviews with Toneka:
contact@tonekaetienne.com

Printed in the United States of America
First printing, 2015
ISBN 978-09967605-2-2
Library of Congress Control Number: 2015951506
Cartienne Publishing, LLC, Atlanta, GA

www.tonekaetienne.com

TABLE OF CONTENTS

ACKNOWLEDGEMENTS

Publisher: Cartienne Publishing, LLC

Book Cover and Interior Design: By Infinite Creations

www.byinfinitecreations.com

Editor: Candice L. Davis

www.gowritesomething.com

Want More?

Looking to connect on a deeper level with the concepts in this book?

Head over to www.toneka.etienne.com/become-you/ and download the Become You FREE Resource Companion.

Book Dedication

To my lovely ladies, Nia Gabrielle and Nadia Simone, you are my heart. Your lives have given me hope and purpose and I hope that my life serves as an example of what can be possible for you.

A CALL TO MY KINDRED

To the one who is frustrated, broken, disappointed, afraid, and tired of letting your dreams die because someone told you it's about sacrifice.

To the one going through the motions, the one who doesn't remember the last time you asked yourself, "What do I want?" You've created a career for yourself, after all the education, and looking at it, you're still not fulfilled. You feel guilty for feeling like it's not enough, like there's still something missing.

That life, that vision, it's here for the taking. You're just looking in all the wrong places. It starts inside, at your root, your soul, and if you dive deep enough, you'll find it. It takes courage, persistence, love, and patience—all for yourself. Yes, and I give you permission. Permission to be bold, scared, vulnerable, alive, honest, whatever you want. Just allow yourself to *be*. And don't worry if you don't know how. I'll hold that space for you to explore; that's why I'm here, what I've been called into your life to do. I'll hold that space for you to be loved, honored, nurtured, supported, and transformed. Are you ready for this? I'll be waiting.

BECOMING ME

Pushing in is sometimes the only way out.

I sat there with a huge lump in my throat. Why was this happening to me? *I take pretty good care of myself. I mean I'm not a saint, but I at least try and eat healthy. Why would this be my diagnosis? Wait, she's kidding, right? I don't have diabetes, not me.* The nurse practitioner showed me the results and proceeded to give me a prescription for a drug to stabilize blood sugar. She also gave me a prescription to pick up a blood glucose meter, a device to keep track of my blood sugar.

I left the office with tears in my eyes, trying my best to remain strong. Once I got in my car, I let it go. I was shaking and crying like a baby. In an instant, my life had been turned upside down. But after all the tears, when I allowed myself to be quiet and listen, a voice said, "Go deeper."

I knew what that meant because I had been asked to go deeper before. In the summer of 2007, my husband, Wesley, and I relocated to the metro Atlanta area with our eight-month-old daughter. I spent the summer enjoying motherhood and getting acclimated to our new surroundings. One night, I was awakened around 3:00 a.m., an hour that would soon become the regular time for my spiritual encounters. I lay still. I don't know how else to explain it, but I knew who it was that wanted my attention. He spoke to my spirit. It was as if He was preparing me. The time He was preparing me for was going to be hard and rough. I could feel it in my spirit. I was scared. But I knew that if I listened and remained close to Him, everything would be fine.

A winter season of my life started in the fall of 2007 and the spring would not arrive until July 2013, almost six years later. During that multi-year cycle, I hit the lowest points of my life, emotionally, spiritually, and physically. By the winter of 2007, I was at the doctor with heart palpitations, stress being the culprit. Full-time work, full-time doctoral pursuit, a young daughter, and another on the way leaves little time for a young married couple. My marriage was suffering tremendously, and I couldn't see a way out of it. Then in 2010, I quit my job, a decision I made because the alternative might have sent me into a nervous breakdown.

It was halftime; this was my chance to take it back into the locker room. I was getting my butt kicked out there! And it was in that moment that I started to go deep. I started to listen to those subtle nudges at 3:00 a.m. He would say things to me like, "Soften," "Listen," "Pray," "Relax,", and "Wait." And I started to pay attention. He had been speaking to me through the world. I just hadn't taken the time to listen. It was in those moments that the world started to come alive, and I was ushered into my purpose. My experiences were no longer the harsh realities of life. They were a catalyst for my own evolution.

By the spring of 2013, my spirit knew that winter was over. I shed my layers, closed the chapter, and for the next six months or so, I just enjoyed life. Then one evening in early 2014, I got the 3:00 a.m. wakeup call again. He said to me, "It's time." I didn't know what that meant, but I shared it with Wesley and told him that I felt like God was ready to use me. In the summer of 2014, when I sat in the doctor's office hearing my diagnosis, it all came back. "Go deeper." This is it. This is what He wants me to do.

After that diagnosis and a few days of self-pity, I pulled out the big guns. I opened the toolbox God planted in me during the winter and used it to heal myself. In the process, I realized that all of the gifts He instilled in me, the experiences I had, all came down to a system, a lifestyle, a way that I approach life. This is my purpose: to inspire, to heal, to listen, to support. It's all encompassing; it requires all of you. But the transformation is deep, it's authentic, it's real, and it's lasting. To get it, you have to go within. It's your only way out.

CHAPTER ONE

---◦◦◦---

Believe

Believe that you were created for a higher purpose.

For years now, I have based my life and anything that I want to build or bring into my life on this Bible verse from Matthew 6:33 (KJV) "But seek ye first the kingdom of God and His righteousness, and all these things shall be added to you." This is a fitting place to ground yourself before embarking on a new endeavor. With the Favor, Grace, and Love of God on my side, I know that things may get difficult along the way, but things will definitely come to pass according to His plan. It's all about alignment and properly establishing Him at the head. So let me start by asking you some questions.

Do you believe you were created for a purpose?

What do you believe about yourself?

What do you believe about your ability to accomplish your dreams, goals, and desires?

The belief system I describe in this book first starts with acknowledging that there is something greater out there in this world operating on your behalf. This can actually be liberating once you think about it. What better feeling could there be than to realize you don't have to accomplish all these amazing dreams and desires you've set out for yourself on your own? In fact, those dreams and desires came from Him. He planted them in you. And since He gave them to you, don't you think He wants to see them come to pass? With the help of a greater power, not only can things be accomplished, but they are always far sweeter, easier, and better than we could have ever imagined. The big dirty secret no one tells you is that you have to first believe.

In her book *A Return to Love,* Marianne Williamson talks about the perfect you, a child of God. She states there's nothing you can do, think, say, or wish that is necessary to establish your worth. In other words, when

God created you, you were already perfect, and there's nothing more for you to do to be worthy of everything this world has to offer. Her statement is about understanding your worth. Worthiness is the fact that you are good enough just the way you are. You were created and put here on Earth for a reason, and because of that fact alone, you are enough—worthy of partaking of all the blessings and favor this life has to offer you, just because.

See, when you really start to internalize this concept, you will recognize that it levels the playing field. There's no one in this world who's better than you or who deserves better things than you because of family, status, job title, or genetic makeup. Nope, I promise you. We are *all* worthy of the same things that this life has to offer. You just have to first *believe* and then *know* that you are worthy of it all.

Unworthiness plays out in our lives all the time. You may hear people making comments about why other people keep receiving so much "blessing," and it's always for some reason that's basically childish and superficial. They'll say things like:

"You know so-and-so got that promotion because she knows the boss's wife."

"They got that new house because their parents gave them the money."

While some of these statements may be true for particular people, it's not the fact that it's true that matters. What matters most is the person who made those statements doesn't believe the same could be true for herself.

Again, this comes down to faith in your own abilities and believing that you're worthy of the same things as anyone else, although they may not come to you the same way they did the other person. And most importantly, it comes down to *you*! For far too long, you've been focused on the wrong things, other people and what's going right in their lives and wrong in your own. Too often, excuses of external things, or things outside of human control, are used to further justify why you can't have the same things. I'm going to challenge you now to turn that mirror on yourself and start to focus on you, the only person you actually have some control over changing.

Once you begin to take in that truth, how does it make you feel? Are you grateful? Has it made you humble? Or maybe it puts you in a place of complete contentment. However it makes you feel the first thing I want you to remember is that now you believe.

We cannot begin this journey together unless we are on the same page, laying a foundation for this pilgrimage of personal evolution. And laying a foundation cannot happen until we are of the same mind. We must first begin with your mindset. But what exactly do I mean by that? Let me further explain to you this complex concept.

In an article written by Sue Mahoney from Texas A&M University, she stated that mindset includes the attitudes and perceptions that we use to interpret the things we encounter in the world. Your mindset is twofold then, attitude and perception. So you must first get your attitude in order. My favorite way to keep my attitude together is through gratitude, but we'll talk more about gratitude in a later chapter. For now, we'll stick to perceptions which play the most influential role in shaping your mindset. Let's look at just how influential they can be. In his book, *Diffusion of Innovations,* Everett Rogers noted that perception can be so influential that, even if you have a great attitude about changing something in your life, your perceived negativity about what that change represents can keep you from accepting that change.

I'm going to use the example of money here because I know we can all relate to that. Who doesn't want more money to come into their life, right? And who doesn't want to get to the point where money is not even an issue and you have more than enough to go around? So you have this great *attitude* about money. You've read all the great books and are ready to implement all the advice. But at your core, your *perception* of money isn't in alignment with that attitude. You still believe that money is evil, that having money is for rich people, and you're not one of those people. You may secretly be scared to have more money because of what it might do to you or your family. In the end, you attract more money into your life, but all that advice you received from books, you don't actually implement. Before you know it, you realize you've continued to do the same things with your money, and nothing has changed!

You can see how, at the end of the day, you might have a great attitude about money, but at your core, your perception of what money represents is still negative and will continue to dictate what you *do* with money.

You see, your perception of things is unconscious and highly complex. You might not even be aware of your perceptions at the moment. But it's your perception that ultimately creates that basis for whether or not you will make a change. I know you've heard the saying "Perception is reality." Well, it really is. And if you want to make some real changes in your life, it's going to require some conscious effort that will likely take time. That's what this book and the process you'll find in it were created to do, make you become more intentional and conscious of your thoughts, feelings, and actions toward change. Please remember, this is a process, not a destination.

Carol Dweck, a professor of psychology at Stanford University, identified two mindsets, fixed and growth. Let's figure out which mindset you subscribe to.

People with a fixed mindset believe that they simply are the way they are. These people usually want to perform well and look smart in front of others. But the way they approach the following things can further explain just how fixed their mindset is.

Challenges

When you have a fixed mindset, you perceive a challenge as a risk, and if you fail, you take on a negative self-image. To avoid the challenge, you'll instead continue to do what you know you do well. In the beginning, I perceived writing this book as a huge risk. Becoming an author is something that I talked about doing as a child, and putting my work and self out there for the whole world to see and judge can be pretty scary. I'm also publishing this book to take steps towards a career as an entrepreneur, but I do have a steady and very comfortable job that, for now, pays my bills.

Can you see why my fixed mindset would cause me to view this career move and writing this book as a risk? I mean, I am successful in my career and have been doing it for a decade now. Why would I want to stop doing that and try something new, something I might fail doing?

Obstacles

When you have a fixed mindset, you'll do your best to avoid obstacles as well. Obstacles are usually external forces that get in the way. The fixed mindset causes you to use these external forces to further validate your reasons why you can't persist. While I was working on my dissertation, I had to fill out this big application and include all the reasons why my study was ethical and wouldn't hurt or harm anyone. I was a good two years into working on this project when I submitted my application to the proper people for review. What I received back looked like a massacre. I had so many corrections to make on this application I became discouraged and completely shut down. This external force was in the way, and I used it as the reason why I couldn't move forward in my process. I didn't even look at the application for over a month.

Effort

When you have a fixed mindset, you see effort as pointless. It holds no weight for you. A fixed mindset will cause you to see effort as something that isn't fun to do and doesn't have a payoff in the end anyway. You'll use this rationale to keep from doing anything. I have to be honest, I've used this rationale for years in an effort to avoid cleaning my house. You know how it goes. You spend several hours getting your house just the way you want it, only to have your husband and kids destroy it soon after. There's nothing worse than spending my time cleaning the kitchen, just to come downstairs the next morning and see dirty dishes in the sink and crumbs all over the table. I got so frustrated that, for the longest, I would shut down and repeat this mantra, "It doesn't matter what I do. No one cares anyway." I saw no payoff in keeping my home clean and tidy, since my mindset told me that no one cared anyway.

Criticism

Negative feedback is either ignored or taken as an insult. Your fixed mindset will cause you to go so far as to believe that the criticism is a direct reflection of yourself. Over time, people around you stop giving you feedback, which further isolates you from forces that could help you create change. Here's an example from my own life. My husband loves to have important conversations full of information in the evenings. That's when I'm my least effective, but he's most effective. I'm a morning person, so by the time 9:00 p.m. rolls around, I can barely remember my name. He's full of energy, and I'm ready to look at the inside of my eyelids!

Things he asked me to do didn't get done because, well, he talked to me at the wrong time. My husband suggested that I needed to write things down because I hadn't been too successful at completing the tasks we needed to do as a family. My fixed mindset made me think, "Really? How you gonna tell me what to do? I'm over here working full time, picking up kids, taking them to activities, doing all the things that mothers do, and I'm still not doing something right?" Because of my fixed mindset, I felt like he was personally attacking me and my capabilities as a woman.

Success of Others

A fixed mindset can make you feel threatened by the success of others. In most cases, you'll reason that the person achieved success from luck or some kind of unacceptable actions. You may go so far as to bring up things about the person that are unrelated to the success. I've been particularly guilty of this. I used to look at these women who have been incredibly successful in their own businesses and think, "Who do they know? What did they do to get so successful?" I would usually attribute their success to them knowing someone famous or just being in the right place at the right time.

By now, I'm sure you've begun to see that a fixed mindset is probably not the most desirable mindset to subscribe to. It creates negativity, isolation, and denial of your own God-given gifts. So let's move on to an affirming mindset, the *growth mindset.*

When you adopt a growth mindset, you view your intelligence and abilities as things that can be developed. Let's examine the way people with a growth mindset approach life.

Challenges

A growth mindset sets you up to perceive a challenge as an opportunity to improve and grow. You see how strong you'll come out on the other side, and you embrace the journey. Let's go back to my earlier example when I faced the dilemma of publishing this book and moving toward a career as an entrepreneur. With a growth mindset, that challenge has become all about my evolution and growth. Becoming an author will not only fulfill a childhood dream of mine, it will also force me to step out of my comfort zone and tackle the journey of trying something new.

Obstacles

When you take on a growth mindset, obstacles, or external setbacks, don't discourage you. You use failure as an opportunity to learn and detach your self-image from your success. This leads you to a win-win attitude in any situation. I would be lying if I said that I didn't take the obstacles in my dissertation application process personally. I had been working my tail off, and to see all those corrections I would have to make was completely demoralizing to my spirit. But one day, it clicked. I thought to myself, "Really, Toneka, this is just part of the process. Suck it up, fix it, and move forward. You need to get done!" That was the moment I detached myself from the red marks on the page, made the necessary changes, and kept it moving.

Effort

A growth mindset allows you to view effort as essential to your personal growth and to mastering new and useful skills in life. To get back to my house cleaning situation, things changed in two ways. First, I matured, and so did my marriage. In the process, I made the effort to express to my husband how unappreciated I felt by his actions after all my hard work. He stepped up and took on more of the responsibility in the house and now makes a conscious effort to applaud me for my contribution. I also take the opportunity to involve my girls in the housework, now that they're older. It not only gives me the opportunity to spend time with them; it also allows me to teach them the importance of cleanliness, responsibility, order, and caring for their living environment. Changing my mindset about the situation didn't only help my marriage; it also gave me more freedom. I was trying to do all the work, but after communicating and teaching, I have three more helpers in the house. I just hooked myself up!

Criticism

When you choose a growth mindset, you choose to view negative feedback as information. You won't always integrate that feedback, and at times, you'll still take it personally. But the difference here is that you'll use this information to improve upon your current abilities. You know, in the end, that you can continue to have an impact on your current situation.

I will admit it's very hard not to take those kinds of things personally, especially when they come in your personal life and you're busting your butt as a wife and mother. But I had to really be honest with myself and use the information my husband gave me to better myself and my situation. So I went back to my strengths and what I know to be true about myself. I communicated with my husband and told him that important information he needs me to remember can't be shared with me late at night. It was just pointless.

My husband is a coach and teacher, and there's always something going on at school. He kept trying to verbally communicate his schedule to me at night, the way I'm least likely to remember information. I used his feedback about my inability to remember what he'd told me and asked him to email me his track and field schedule for the season. Once I see something and get it on my calendar, I can remember it, and better yet, plan accordingly.

Something as simple as that adjustment has improved our communication and coordination of schedules. Now, the minute he gets any work-related emails with important dates, my husband forwards them right to me, and I put them right on my calendar.

Success of Others

A growth mindset gives you the confidence to see the success of others as a source of encouragement, information, and inspiration. You study and find the lessons in the success of others and use them to propel you forward. This couldn't describe more accurately where I am right now on my journey. I love to see other women succeed, and I am constantly reading about and studying women more successful than I am to inspire me and move me forward.

Can you see some definite differences between the two mindsets? I'm sure you know by now which mindset you need to subscribe to in order to knock your goals out the park, right? The biggest difference between the two comes down to a matter of *choice.* You have a choice in how you perceive the challenges and obstacles in your life. If you noticed, the growth mindset requires you to take *responsibility* for yourself and view potential negatives as *opportunities.* This is going to be essential as you move forward because we all know that life can get difficult at times. But with the right mindset, you can be sure to win.

CHAPTER TWO

———)( )(———

Evaluate

*Evaluation of self allows you to pit your current reality against
the one you desire.*

Now that you've spent time dealing with your mindset, it's time to get out of your head and look at what's going on in your life on a daily basis. Evaluating yourself will reveal to you if, in fact, your perception of yourself aligns with the reality of the choices you make and of your behavior, which ultimately affects how successful you are at accomplishing the things you set out to do. The goal of this next section is for you to conduct a life audit for yourself. In this life audit, you will be given strategies and resources to identify your strengths, review and honestly take a look at the habits that are either helping or hurting your daily life, evaluate your current lifestyle, and reach outside of yourself and poll friends and family to give you a different perspective.

Our society focuses so much on all of the negative attributes of a person. Particularly in my field of psychology and counseling, there is an emphasis on pinpointing problems in people and attaching a name or diagnosis to describe them. Although this style of evaluation has some merit, I prefer to focus on the strengths of an individual as a starting point. Making the decision to improve yourself is already a vulnerable process, so the last thing I want to do is remind you of all the parts of your life that still could use some improvement. So let's start with the good.

Now when I talk about your strengths, I'm talking about those personality traits that exist within you and extend across all areas of your life. The way to identify them is to look for patterns in your life, areas in which you realize you do the same things and, most importantly, you do them well. You may be the person who your friends and family come to when they have financial problems and need some guidance, or maybe you're the mediator between family members when a familial conflict arises. Finally, take a look at the things in your life that you enjoy doing because they likely will lead you to identifying your strengths. Below, I provide an example of my own evaluation and how I came to identify some of my strengths.

I noticed a pattern in my own life. Both friends and family often called me up to sort out problems they were having a hard time making sense of. This could vary from something as simple as how to get their young child on a schedule to which route to take when choosing a new career.

Activity that I enjoy: Helping friends and family sort through difficult situations in their lives

Is this activity mental, physical, or both? This activity is a mental activity.

What skills does the activity require: When I'm talking to people, I notice that I have to be a good listener, patient and empathetic. When listening to their dilemmas, I evaluate all possible scenarios of a situation, and can see potential pros and cons. I use this information to help me explain their options, give my own opinion, and then leave the decision to them.

How do I feel when I'm doing this activity? I feel confident, helpful, and grateful that I was chosen to help them.

Synopsis of strength: One of my strengths is that I am a strategic thinker. I evaluate all possible scenarios of a situation, can see potential pros and cons in multiple situations, and use all of this information before I make a decision about something.

The strength I identified doesn't just help me in one area of my life. It's what I call a *holistic strength,* which I started to apply in all areas of my life. But how else can you identify your holistic strengths? Another great way to identify your strengths is to determine what kind of learning style fits you best: auditory, kinesthetic, or visual. Everyone processes and learns information differently, and determining which way or ways you learn best can help you to leverage your time and determine optimal ways to learn and take in new information, which in turn, helps you to become better at achieving your goals.

Auditory learners retain information most effectively through hearing and speaking. These learners often prefer to be told *how* to do things and will then summarize the main points aloud to help with retention. These individuals often have musical talents, are great speakers, and retain information best with soft music playing in the background.

Visual learners, on the other hand, use visual objects, such as pictures, graphs, and charts, to help facilitate learning. They are good at reading body language and remember things best when they write them down. These learners excel by thinking in pictures and creating mental images to retain information.

Finally, kinesthetic learners use the hands-on approach when learning new information. They're generally good at demonstrating how to do something rather than explaining it. They have a good sense of balance and hand-eye coordination, and they remember and process information when interacting with the environment around them.

Use the Learning Styles Assessment to determine which style(s) best fits you. If you would rather take this assessment with pen and paper, head over to http://www.tonekaetienne.com/become-you/ and download your FREE Become You Resource Companion.

Learning Styles Assessment

1. When I learn something new, it's best that I:

    a. watch someone show me how to do it

    b. hear someone tell me how to do it

    c. try to do it myself

2. When I have to concentrate or study something, I:

    a. focus on the words or pictures

    b. talk about the problem and the possible solutions in my head

    c. move around often and touch things

3. When waiting, I typically:

    a. look around, stare, or read

    b. talk or listen to others

    c. walk around, use my hands, or shake my feet while seated

4. When making a choice about purchasing something, I tend to:

    a. read as much as I can about the product

    b. listen to recommendations from friends

    c. test out the new product

5. When I have to solve a problem, I:

    a. write or draw diagrams to see it

    b. talk myself through it

    c. use my entire body or move objects to help me think

6. I most enjoy:

    a. watching movies, photography, or people watching

    b. listening to music or having conversations with friends

    c. participating in sporting activities, eating out, or dancing

7. If I have to remember a list of things, I remember if best if I:

    a. write them down

    b. repeat them over and over to myself

    c. move around and used my body to remember each item

8. If I'm unhappy with physical items I purchased, I find it easiest to:

    a. write out my complaints in a letter, text, or email

    b. discuss it with a representative over the phone

    c. take the item back to the store

9. In school, I prefer teachers who:

    a. use a board, overhead projector, or lecture notes while they teach

    b. talk with lots of expression

    c. use hands on activities

10. When buying clothes, I choose them based mostly on:

    a. their colors and how they look

    b. how the salespeople describe the clothes to me

    c. their textures and how the clothes feel on me

11. When trying to recall someone I've met, I remember:

    a. faces, but forget names

    b. names, but forget faces

    c. the situation in which I met the person

12. When I give directions, I tend to:

    a. see the actual places in my mind or prefer to draw them

    b. have no difficulty giving them verbally

    c. have to point or move my body while I give the directions

13. I am most drawn to people based on:

a. how they look

b. what they say to me

c. how they make me feel

14. I spend most of my free time:

a. watching movies or TV

b. talking with friends

c. participating in some physical activity or making things

15. When I get upset, I tend to:

a. re-play the scenario in my mind

b. raise my voice to let people know how upset I am

c. stomp, slam doors, and physically show people my anger

Scoring Instructions: Add the number of responses for each letter. The letter with the most responses is your primary learning style. You will likely have a preferred learning style, with a blend or mixture of two. Please know, there are no right or wrong learning styles, just the learning style(s) that works best for you.

a = visual learning style

b = auditory learning style

c = kinesthetic learning style

Below are several techniques to make the most of each learning style.

If you are a visual learner:

•   Avoid visual distractions, such as windows or doorways when you have to complete a task.

•   Focus on big concepts first, like paying off debt or getting that bathroom remodeled; then break those big concepts down into bite sized steps.

•   Keep a notebook and pen with you; if someone tells you important information, ask them to repeat it while you write it down.

(Remember my example from chapter one. I talked about my need to write down information that my husband gives me. My preferred learning style is visual, and I keep a notebook in every room of my house.)

•   You are the list person, so take advantage and use to-do lists to help you accomplish your daily goals.

•   Ask someone to demonstrate or *show* you how to do something; you need to *see* it done.

If you are an auditory learner:

•   Use soft, wordless background music when completing tasks.

•   Use a recorder from your phone to capture important information and play it back for yourself.

•   Converse with people as much as possible to remember things.

•   Ask some to *tell* you something rather than write it down or show you.

•   After being *told* something, repeat it back in your own words for better understanding.

If you are a kinesthetic learner:

•   Complete tasks by taking frequent breaks so you can move your body.

•   Take in new information while doing an activity such as listening to an audio book while on a treadmill.

•   Choose activities that allow you to demonstrate your knowledge through movement, demonstration, or field experience.

•   Ask people to keep instructions short and to the point.

•   Use your skills to teach others how to do what you know.

Lastly, identify your strengths by asking family and friends to give their opinion. Choose individuals whose perspective you value and who you trust will give you an honest answer. You could do something as simple as sending out the following text: "Hey ____! I am in the process of doing some self-improvement in my life, and it was suggested that I complete this quick exercise. I would really love your help. What three words would you use to best describe me?"

It's that simple. If you'd like to take it a step further, I suggest replying with three words for them as well. This is a great way to reciprocate the positive energy and can provide an instant boost of confidence for both you and your helper. This exercise helped me to validate my own strengths and also gave me insight and validated how others perceived me. You want to make sure that what you're putting out there in the world aligns with your own vision for yourself. Are you finding this to be the case, or are you way off?

I read all the time when I was younger, and sometime in my early teens, I read about what it meant to be ambidextrous, the ability to use both left and right hands well. I learned that it meant that you could use both sides of your brain, which isn't the norm for most people. The average person tends to have a dominant side of the brain.

The inquisitive part of me was fascinated and totally sold on the idea of making both sides of my brain equally strong. See, I was a psychologist back then and didn't even know it. I get a thrill out of testing theories and love to be outside the norm, so I set out to make myself ambidextrous.

I started off by trying to practice writing with my left hand every day, since I'm right handed. This wasn't exactly the easiest thing to do. Writing my name took at least five minutes, and don't even try and ask me to write in cursive. Oh, lord! So I pivoted and decided try to use my left hand during an activity that I do every day, eating.

I'm a daddy's girl, so when we went out to a restaurant to eat, I always wanted to sit next to my father. He's left-handed, and once our food came, our elbows would get in a sword fight as we started to eat since I was right-handed and he a lefty. So I switched over to my left hand, which made it easier for us both. Initially it was a deliberate decision I made, but over time, it became something I didn't think about, and I naturally started to eat with my left hand. Today, I still eat with my left hand, although I may change every now and then to accommodate someone. My habit started as something deliberate and turned into an unconscious act.

Habits are learned behavioral patterns involving a three-part process. The first part is a cue or trigger that tells your brain to begin the process of letting a behavior unfold. Second, is the routine, or the behavior itself. Last, is the reward, or something that makes your brain look forward to performing the three-part process again in the future. In other words, an action becomes a habit the moment the behavior goes from being conscious to unconscious. If you noticed in my example above, my cue to use my left hand was sitting down to eat. The actual routine was using my left hand during the meal, and the reward was twofold, being more like my father and developing both sides of my brain.

Neuroscientists have identified a part of your brain called the basal ganglia as the habit-forming culprit, due to its connection to memories, emotions, and pattern formation. As a habit becomes automatic, other parts of the brain don't have to work as hard and shut down. This is where the basal ganglia takes over and starts to perform this task for you, and you go on auto-pilot. These kind of automatic behaviors are performed the same way, every time, in the same environment. Pay attention to the steps you go through the next time you brush your teeth or take a shower. It's likely you do them the same way every day. However, if you take a vacation, your habit will likely change. This is why it's a good idea to break a habit while on vacation, because your cues and patterns are broken.

On the one hand, it's empowering to know your brain has the ability to create a behavior in you that can become unconscious and which you can perform daily without much brain power. That's great if those habits are serving you, but what about those habits that are actually keeping you from being your best? We'll talk in later chapters about how to intentionally change them. But for now, let's assess your daily lifestyle.

Life Audit

Let me be clear. You're still in the life-evaluation phase, so please don't feel the need to change anything yet. This part is about acknowledging and identifying everything you do, the good and the bad. I'm not talking about passing judgment on yourself. This is about getting brutally honest with yourself about your daily lifestyle choices. As you start to track and write down what you do on a daily basis, this record will become the lens to focus your attention on reality instead of your *perception* of your reality. You need to shed light on the realities of your lifestyle choices if you really want to make a change for the better.

I've divided the major parts of your lifestyle into six areas:

1.   Spirituality

2.   Career and work

3.   Relationships

4.   Exercise, nutrition, and wellness

5.   Personal development

6.   Finances

For each of the areas, evaluate where you fall on a scale of one (imbalance) to ten (balance). Answer the following questions to help you further evaluate your current reality in each area of your lifestyle.

Spirituality

Questions to consider:

•   Do I have a consistent spiritual practice in my life right now?

•   How do I integrate my spirituality into my life?

•   Do I use my spirituality as a barometer while navigating through life? Why or why not?

Career and Work

Questions to consider:

• Do I have a career that is satisfying to me?

• Is my career allowing me to use my gifts and strengths to their fullest potential?

• Do I actively seek opportunities to grow professionally?

Relationships

Questions to consider:

• Do I have satisfying relationships in my life right now (e.g. marriage, significant other, family, friends, etc.)?

• Do I put time in to nurturing and maintaining those relationships?

• Do I actively seek opportunities to establish new relationships?

Exercise, Nutrition, and Wellness

Questions to consider:

- Am I physically active at least two times a week?

- Do I eat healthy foods that nourish my body?

- Do I routinely see a healthcare provider for preventative care?

Personal Development

Questions to consider:

- Am I actively making choices to improve my life every day?

- Do I seek new opportunities to grow and get out of my comfort zone?

- Do I feel like my life is moving in the direction I want it to?

Finances

Questions to consider:

- Am I able to comfortably afford my expenses?

• Can I make better decisions about what I do with my money?

• Do I have a plan for my money *before* it comes to me?

So how did it turn out for you? You'll likely find that you could stand to improve in all of these areas, but for now, I suggest focusing on one. You have the opportunity to apply the strategy laid out below again in the future with other areas. In order to facilitate maximum success during this process, hone in on the area that's most important to you right now. Once you've chosen your area, here are some additional questions to answer:

• What does a 10 (balance) in this area look like to me? Be specific.

• Why is it important for me to create more balance in this area?

• What changes will I have to implement to make this area a 10?

- Which mindset category(ies) has me the most hung up in this area, *challenges, obstacles, effort, criticism, or the success of others?* (Review the fixed and growth mindset discussion from chapter one.)

- What feelings or emotions do I experience when thinking about this area?

- What do I need to learn or ask for in order to make it a 10?

Here is an example of how these questions can be answered:

Claire, a busy wife and mother of two young children, completes this exercise and comes up with the following:

Spirituality = 8

Career and Work = 7

Relationships = 5

Exercise, Nutrition, and Wellness = 3

Personal Development = 7

Finances = 7

She decides that she will focus her attention on creating more balance in the exercise, nutrition and wellness area of her life. Here are her responses to the questions:

•   What does a 10 (balance) in this area look like to me? Be specific.

Ultimate balance in my exercise/nutrition/wellness area would include a consistent exercise regimen consisting of approximately three days each week of exercise, such as walking, jogging, yoga, swimming, and weight training. I will have established healthy eating habits by planning out most of my meals and bringing my lunch to work most days. As a result of these good habits, I will no longer be on high blood pressure medication, and I will maintain a healthy weight for my age and height.

•   Why is it important for me to create more balance in this area?

It's important for me to create this balance because I have a family history of heart disease, diabetes, and high blood pressure, and I don't want to become dependent on medication like so many of my family members. I also have two young children who I need to be healthy for, and I want to pass on good habits to them. Finally, this balanced lifestyle will give me more confidence in my physical appearance, which will help me feel more comfortable in my marriage.

• What changes will I have to implement to make this area a 10?

I will have to change my eating habits, giving up fast food and frozen dinners, which are generally my primary means of eating. I will also have to decide how I'm going to get my exercise in, which may require me to get up earlier in the morning to work out before the kids wake up.

• Which mindset category(ies) has me the most hung up in this area, challenges, obstacles, effort, criticism, or the success of others?

I've been allowing obstacles and effort to be my primary hang-ups. Because I do the primary care giving,

I've used the excuses that I'm tired and don't have the money to find a babysitter for the kids. I have also tried the healthy eating and exercise thing before, and it hasn't worked in the past, so why will it work this time around?

• What feelings or emotions do I experience when thinking about this area?

I get frustrated and feel overwhelmed. I've dieted so much in the past, and I haven't been able to make healthy eating a permanent fixture in my life. I feel like a failure because I'm now twenty pounds overweight and don't feel pretty. It feels so hard and takes so much effort to make this happen, and I don't want to disappoint my husband or myself. We have our wedding anniversary coming up in six months, and I want to feel confident, sexy, and beautiful when we go on our beach vacation.

• What do I need to learn or ask for in order to make it a 10?

I need to learn how to manage portions when eating. I also need to learn how to eat every three hours, like my doctor suggested. I am going to research different gyms in my area, to see if they have daycare for the kids, and look at also possibly doing some workouts at home early in the morning. I'm also going to ask my husband to cheer me on and pick up the slack in the house so that I can make this a priority. Finally, I'm going to ask a few girlfriends if they will join me so we can hold each other accountable.

Working through these questions and being honest with where you are, where you want to be, and what you're going to have to do to get you there can really create a transformative moment for you. I encourage you to actually write out the answers to these questions and not just leave them up there in your head. There is power in getting things down on paper. It all becomes more real when you see it in front of you. Just make sure you do it without judgment of yourself. We all have our things to work on. This just happens to be *your* thing.

CHAPTER THREE

—•( )•—

Create

Create life systems for maximum ease and efficiency

W e've made it to the midway point, and now it's time to be creative, my favorite part! You've spent time grounding yourself in your own belief system and what you know to be true about yourself, and you even took the intentional action of evaluating your own life by completing the life audit. Now it's time to *create* that life that you've always envisioned for yourself. But this time, you're doing so while standing in your own truth and understanding the mindsets and behaviors that got you so far from your purpose. Remember this book is here to help you to uncover your strengths and, at the same time, be honest with the mindsets and behaviors that have held you back thus far. Now it's time to use what you've learned to create a lifestyle customized for you.

Structure and Discipline

The concept of discipline often gets a bad rap because it so often is associated with doing something wrong. It also implies that you have to be corrected, or you need to be fixed. But when we talk about discipline in terms of disciplining ourselves so that we can experience freedom, discipline then becomes about creating systems, structures, and parameters in your life that you operate within. Because when you have structure and discipline in your life, it creates a sense of confidence, freedom, and security.

I have two young daughters, and as a busy mother, it can be really hard to remember to have my ladies complete their chores. So I write out every task I need my ladies to complete in the morning as they're preparing to go to school. I put these tasks on a dry erase easel board in their bedroom, with check boxes next to each task. I even color-code them in their favorite colors. Some of the tasks included: making their beds, brushing their teeth, and getting lunches in book bags. You get the picture. What I noticed is that the girls *loved* the satisfaction that came with completing each of their tasks. They hurried to complete each one so that they could put that check in the box.

Completing all the tasks before leaving the house was a personal victory for each of my ladies, as well as for me. With this system, I encouraged them to develop their reading skills by changing up the vocabulary on the lists. This strategy for having them complete their chores on their own trained them to follow directions, instilled personal responsibility in them, and encouraged their independence, building up their confidence.

On the parent end of things, I freed up my own time in the mornings to focus on myself, confident that my ladies would handle their own business. I disciplined my daughters by creating a structured system for them to follow, which gave them a sense of freedom, security, and confidence. These hallmarks of healthy child development were more easily achieved since children thrive in structured environments. They feel secure because they know what to expect and the expectation is consistently delivered.

As an adult, you need to take that same philosophy and apply it to your own life. We tend to think that we should be free of that kind of structure and discipline after a certain age, free to make our own decisions. But the more of "my own thing" that I tried to do, the more I realized I wasn't moving forward toward accomplishing anything. However, when I started to become more strategic about how I approached my own life, I no longer woke up in the mornings with uncertainty or worried about how the day was going to go. I put a structure in place and told myself the things I was going to do. Once I started to do this, my days became more productive, and I was more confident and made significant progress. The structure is not to put you in a box. Structure and discipline are meant to give you a way to be safe and accountable and to honor yourself and the things you want to do. Look, you've got big things to accomplish in your life, and you have no time to just wing it. It's imperative that you embrace structure and discipline in your life.

Systems

One simple way to begin to create the kind of life you desire is to create systems to become more efficient and save time. You've likely already created systems in your life, though you may not carry out all the steps or have truly optimized the effectiveness of your systems. Simply put, systems include anything that happens regularly in your life, things like errands, laundry, and, grocery shopping. The best way to create or discover a system is to examine those repeated actions you do for a particular task.

Not sure where to start? Begin with a task, and make a list of every action step you have to do to complete it. The next time you set out to do that task, pull out your checklist and follow the steps. Missing steps? Just add them to your list and you've just created your first system! Let's examine this case study of Bianca's life and create a system customized just for her.

On Monday, Bianca needs to do some grocery shopping, so she goes to the grocery store. When she gets home, she realizes she forgot to buy milk, so on Tuesday, she purchases the milk and makes a stop at the dry cleaners to drop off some clothes. On Wednesday, she realizes she forgot to drop off her favorite black pants at the cleaners, so she drops those off during her lunch break. After work, she picks up some dog food on the way home. On Thursday, after work, Bianca makes three different stops to pick up supplies for a party she plans to host on Friday evening.

Can you see how Bianca created a very chaotic and stressful life for herself? Let's see how a simple system put in place for Bianca can make her life more efficient.

First, Bianca makes a decision that Saturdays will be her day to complete all errands and grocery shopping. She even gives this system a name, *Weekend Rendezvous Roundup!* The entire week leading up to Saturday, Bianca keeps two separate lists, an errand list and a grocery list. She plans ahead for the following two weeks of errands and grocery shopping. She plans out her route based on stops she has to make: grocery, cleaners, and pet store.

Once Saturday arrives, Bianca spends two hours of her time completing her *Weekend Rendezvous Roundup*, which saves her both time and money. Since she's planned efficiently, she saves gas and multiple trips around town. Bianca also takes her strengths into consideration when creating this system. She's a visual learner, so lists work well for her, and she's a morning person, so she completes her system on a Saturday morning, all before noon.

Here are some things to consider when creating your own system:

• Give your system a name. This creates ownership and formalizes the process.

• Make sure you write down the system, step by step, and post it somewhere.

• Designate a day and time for your system. This will give that structure and discipline to your life.

- Group things, if possible, to maximize time and money.

- Stick to the system.

- Reevaluate the system; the system may need some tweaking or require some changes in your lifestyle. For example, Saturday morning errands are out of the question for me from February to May. My husband is a track coach, and that's when track meets are scheduled.

What if you don't have a system for a process? Ask friends and family, and see what they do. Try on their systems for a while, and tweak them to fit you. Systems are a great way to make your life run smoothly and effortlessly. Take advantage of the people around you who are already experiencing success in an area you wish to improve in. Remember the growth mindset from chapter one? Take note of the lessons of others who have found success, and use them as a source of inspiration.

Routines

Now that we've looked at systems and how best to identify and create them in your own life for maximum efficiency, what happens if you want to integrate a new habit into your daily system? Well, the best way to do this is to evaluate your routines and then integrate a new cue within the routine to create a lasting habit. Let me explain further. In their article about habit formation from the University College of London, Lally, Wardle, and Gardner stated that implementing a new action or habit in your everyday routine increases the likelihood that you will continue to repeat this new habit, which will then lead to making this habit permanent. Zacks, Speer, Swallow, Braver, & Reynolds further validated this concept with the introduction of their theory, Event Segmentation Theory or EST, a theory developed at Washington University in St. Louis, Missouri. EST states that there are certain points in an existing routine that provide the best time to start a new behavior. The theory suggests that in order to make a new habit permanent, the most effective thing to do is to place a cue *within* the already established routine, rather than *preceding* the routine. So what is all this mumbo jumbo really saying? Let's go through a scenario to make this more practical.

William has been trying for months to establish a consistent flossing routine in his daily life. For the past year, his dentist has been urging him to make flossing a priority. As a result of his inability to floss consistently, William was told he had three cavities at his last dentist appointment. He has decided that flossing will have to become a non-negotiable in his daily life, and he turns to his routine to help him create this new habit.

Upon review, William recalls his brushing regimen, breaking it down into specific steps.

1. Pick up toothbrush and toothpaste.

2. Put toothpaste on toothbrush.

3. Turn on faucet and wet the toothbrush.

4. Proceed to brush teeth and tongue.

5. Rinse mouth and toothbrush and return toothbrush to its holder.

6. Pour mouthwash into mouth and rinse.

7. Put mouthwash back.

8. Dry face and hands with towel.

If you recall, EST recommends placing the cue to establish the new habit *within* an already established routine. So in the case of William's teeth-brushing regimen, he chooses to place the cue right at the end of step five. Returning his toothbrush to its holder will serve as the cue to pick up the floss. After flossing, William will continue steps six, seven, and eight, like he always has. According to the theory, this is the most effective way to integrate a new habit into a routine. This way is found to be more effective than attempting to place flossing at the *beginning* of the regimen.

By now you likely have some practical strategies in place to help you create the kind of lifestyle you desire. This kind of work doesn't happen without discipline and structure and being intentional when creating systems and routines that support you. But what happens when we get these systems into place and still feel stuck? Let's explore some obstacles that may be stifling your evolution.

CHAPTER FOUR

Obstacles

Obstacles are just speed bumps on the road to enlightenment.

I started working on my PhD in the fall of 2007. My husband and I had secured new full-time jobs and moved to metro Atlanta one month earlier, with our eight-month-old daughter in tow. From the outside looking in, this goal looked like a pretty lofty one, working on a doctorate degree while working full time and fulfilling my roles as wife and mother to a husband and a young infant. But for me, those first two and a half years of coursework were, for lack of better words, a piece of cake. I had a certain mindset, a focus that was unshakable. I also had this unexplainable confidence about myself, which proved to give me an advantage at the perfect time.

Approximately two and half years into my program, I traveled to Minneapolis for a residency, during which we were encouraged to begin the search for our dissertation chairs. The dissertation, an extremely long piece of writing with lots of research, usually required to obtain your doctorate degree, was the final piece of the puzzle to complete my doctorate. There are several procedures and processes in place to walk you through the creation of this extensive body of research. The first step is to secure a dissertation chair, or someone who takes the responsibility of guiding you through the process. I quickly perused the list of potential professors who shared similar research interests with me and settled on one name. She was not only an accomplished researcher, she happened to be the Dean of the School of Psychology.

I signed up to have a one-on-one consultation with her during the residency, knowing that this would be my time to pitch her my research proposal and ask her if she would be my chair. I sat down in front of her, full of excitement, and proceeded to tell her my research interest, African American mothers and daughters. Looking back, I really had no idea what I was talking about. I could barely articulate to her what my research ultimately entailed, but one thing I emphatically stated to her, "I have chosen *you* to be my chair." She laughed, and I'm sure she was taken aback, since students do not typically *tell* professors what they're going to do. But I had an undeniable confidence in myself and knew that, with her in my corner, I could get this degree completed. She gave me a tentative yes and required me to submit a proposal to her that evening. I spent at least three hours that night working on it, but once I submitted it to her, the deal was sealed, and the rest is history.

Just two short months later, that undeniable confidence was no more, and I was stuck. Two and half years of coursework had culminated in me standing at the bottom of yet another mountain, the dissertation. The U.S. Department of Education has estimated that the average doctorate attrition rate is between 40 to 50 percent. Of those 40 to 50 percent, African Americans earned only 6.1 percent of the doctorates awarded in the 2006 – 2007 academic school year, despite making up 13 percent of the population. Can you see how the odds were stacked against me? Of course, knowing all of this information prior to beginning my doctorate journey didn't exactly help me, and I reached a point that everything came crashing down. I was completely overwhelmed. Fear inevitably set in.

Fear

Fear is a crippling little monster, isn't it? It can stop you dead in your tracks and keep you from moving forward in life. I've used fear over and over in my life to justify not doing or completing things, but the more I started to understand fear, the more empowered I became. In the last two chapters, you got out of your head and looked at all of the things you can *see* in your life. Now it's time to get back in your head and understand more about how your thoughts can affect your actions. Educating yourself about the things you don't understand actually creates a sense of empowerment.

Once I started to understand fear, I realized it's a feeling that can serve as a catalyst to move forward, in spite of the way it makes me feel. Am I saying that I'm never fearful? No. But what I do now is to continue to move forward in spite of the fear. It's an uncomfortable feeling, but once you move past it, there's a plethora of better feelings on the other side. So let's explore the types of fears that creep up and try to sabotage our lives.

The *fear of failure* assumes that you will not succeed, so instead of pressing forward you give up. But let me offer a different perspective. Failing is and should be a part of life. It's a barometer to let you know that at least you're trying. Here's the truth: you don't have to think of any experience (no matter how upsetting or disappointing it may be) as a failure. It's not. It's simply a redirection. Timing is everything, and sometimes you have to be patient and wait your turn.

Fear of success is a very real fear that creeps up mostly when you're really trying to create some lasting change in your life. What's even more difficult with this fear is that it's hard to gauge because it relies so heavily on the future, which is something you're unable to control. This is why it is so important to create a very detailed and vivid visualization of your future. Once you start to create it yourself, there's no need to be afraid. You know what's going to happen.

The *fear of uncertainty* is really the definition of life. I mean, you don't know what could happen to you from day to day, so the best thing to do is get comfortable with being uncomfortable. But how do you do that? Ditch the lofty expectations and focus on what *you* can control to create the desired outcomes. You have to stop expecting the world and other people to live up to these expectations you place on them. Instead, focus on *creating* what you desire. It's all on you.

Fear of rejection can stop people from forming relationships, trying out a new hobby, or asking for that promotion. Again, this comes down to a growth mindset and the realization that you can only do your part and detach yourself from the outcome. It's common for people who feel unworthy to not ask for more, but if you value yourself and your abilities, ask away! The real power is in the *ask*. When you ask for what you want, you're affirming to yourself and the world that you're worthy of it. How empowering is that? Does this mean you'll always get what you want? No. But it will serve to increase your confidence and energy, and what is yours will be yours.

Finally, *fear of change* happens when you're afraid to leave your comfort zones. One of the best ways to combat this fear is to simply embrace excitement. There's something better coming your way, and that's definitely something to be excited about, right? So allow that emotion to push you forward rather than stop you. Also, now is the time to seek out wisdom from others who have gone before you. You can ask them what they did to get them through and what they would have done differently. Last, focus on the things that are constant in your life, such as friends and family. This will serve as your safe place and remind you that not everything in your life is changing.

Procrastination

Procrastinating is the art of actively postponing or delaying something. And it's just another one of the obstacles that can potentially stand in the way of living the life of your dreams. But did you know there are different kinds of procrastinators? See if you fit into one of the following categories.

1.   *Thrill-seeker* - These are usually your last minute, "get it done" kind of people. They wait until the last minute to complete an important task or project and attribute their procrastination to their "zone of genius." I am very guilty of embodying this one right here. I spent the majority of graduate school being a thrill-seeker. I would wait until the weekend before a huge paper was due and spend the next day and a half writing around the clock to get it done. This form of procrastination always caused me a great deal of self-inflicted stress, and after finishing an assignment, I'd always promise myself I wasn't going to do it again.

2.   *The Avoider* - This person usually procrastinates by avoiding the task and usually does so out of either fear of success or fear of failure. This one crept up for me as I was writing this book. So many times while thinking about this book, I thought, "No one wants to hear what you have to say." I also thought about how the success of this book

could change my life, which brought up some fears that I didn't realize I had.

3.   *The Indecisive* - This person can't and won't make a decision. Unfortunately, even with her lack of action, she still won't take responsibility for her outcomes. Very rarely does this type of procrastinator believe she has any responsibility for her life, and she presents herself as a victim in most situations.

So how can you combat procrastination?

Break it down. You can get really overwhelmed by a complex task or project. Sometimes you may have a project you want to tackle, but once you start to think about all the pieces of the puzzle, it gets all too daunting. At that point, you can either turn into the avoider or the indecisive. So instead of looking at the project as this huge mountain of a task, break it down in steps.

That was one of the things that helped me to complete my dissertation. I focused on one chapter at a time and didn't allow myself to even think about steps 2 through

100! Here's another great tip if you're still stuck: start at either the beginning or the end and fill in the pieces along the way. I almost never know exactly how something I write is going to turn out. I start with just one section, and it develops from there. You just have to trust the process and take it one step at a time.

Reward yourself. As I stated before, I can be the thrill-seeker type of procrastinator, since I get so emotionally charged up about the things I have to do. So to add some spice to the mix, I put myself on a reward system to get things done. I give myself a deadline to complete something, and if I do it on schedule, I treat myself to something that I know I'll enjoy. I started with very simple rewards, like an extra scoop of ice cream or a new necklace. I realized that when I procrastinated, this dark cloud remained over me, and I couldn't enjoy my leisure time. So I started to reward myself with things like more family time, an afternoon at the park with my girls, or a date night with my husband. I've mentioned breaking down your tasks. You don't have to complete the huge task to reward yourself. Instead, implement little rewards along the way. While writing this book, I would give myself short tasks to complete a section, knowing that if I did so, the weekend time I spent with my family would be that much more rewarding and pleasurable since I'd knocked something off my list.

Reframe. Sometimes you get so wrapped up in your emotions and fears that you forget why you started on this journey in the first place. To reframe is to connect back to your *why*, it's your reminder of what's most important. When you connect to the driving force behind your journey, allow that force to propel you forward in spite of the temptation of procrastination.

Disconnect. Eliminate all possible distractions to create your work environment. Turn off the cell phone and television. Create a clean work space—whatever you need to do to help you focus and get to work. When I go into serious creation mode, I have to completely remove myself from any familiar environments. While finishing my dissertation, I spent two and a half days locked in a hotel room. I wrote, ate, slept, repeat. And it worked for me, I completed two of my five chapters. And for this book, I took the same approach. For three days, I focused all my attention on this book, in a hotel room, with tiny rewards along the way. I rewarded myself with a brownie one night, a hot tub party with my husband and daughters in the hotel another night, and a new bathing suit the last night.

Negative Thought Patterns

Fear is often the trigger that sends your thoughts and emotions down the spiraling black hole of negative thought patterns. As I've stated before, our thoughts and emotions are extremely powerful and dictate our actions, so it's incredibly important, while on the path of self-discovery and self-improvement, to identify negative thought patterns when they start to rear their ugly heads. Here are several negative thought patterns that you may fall victim to.

The Know-It-All

This thought pattern assumes that you already know how people feel about you, and it's usually all negative.

"I know they wouldn't hire me anyway, so I won't bother applying for that job."

The Emotional Basket Case

A person with this thought pattern allows her emotions to dictate her thinking and behavior and how she perceives the world.

"I *feel* like I'm not smart enough to get another degree, so I must not be smart."

Everyone's Stupid Except Me

When you fall victim to this thought pattern, you tend to see people as less competent than they really are.

"My husband can't clean the house as well as I can, so I'll go behind him and fix what he's done so it's correct."

Jumping to Conclusions

When you jump to conclusions, you make conclusions without evidence to back up your assumptions.

"She's dressed way too fancy, so she must be stuck up, shallow, and full of Botox."

All My Fault

When you indulge in this thought pattern, you view yourself as the cause of everything bad that's happened to you. At the same time, you're also unlikely to take credit for all the good in your life.

"It's my fault he cheated on me."

Life is Crap

This negative thought pattern convinces you that everything and everyone is bad, no one can be trusted, and nothing good will happen in your life.

"I've never had much, I won't have much, and the way society is going, we're all going to kill each other anyway."

These negative thought patterns create a negative inner dialogue that you have with yourself before you even utter a word or *do* anything. So my challenge to you is to monitor that inner dialogue. Notice how those negative thoughts illicit negative emotions and feelings, which ultimately can have detrimental effects on your *actions*.

Here's a trick. At the onset of negative inner dialogue, just observe it. Don't try to change it. Imagine it as a word passing by on a giant cloud in your mind. In the other clouds are more positive inner dialogues. You have the choice of which one to believe and internalize as your truth. This is your gentle reminder that your thoughts are *in* you but don't have to *be* you. This is about creating the life you desire, and it starts with what you believe, and what you think, to be true of yourself and others.

CHAPTER FIVE

───────◦( )◦───────

Manifest

To manifest is to present one's dreams with the anticipation that they will become reality.

Throughout my own self-discovery journey, getting my mindset together and then taking action that was in alignment with that mindset has been about 50% of the formula to my success. So what do you think is the other 50%? This is the last, and dare I say, most important component to this trinity of concepts: manifesting. I place the art of manifesting, or activating universal laws that are already there in the universe, in the spiritual or soulful category and believe it to be that icing on the cake, that important piece of the puzzle, when it comes to self-discovery and true transformation. When used in conjunction with your growth mindset and inspired action, manifesting and all its components add a powerful layer to your journey.

The Law of Abundance

Nevertheless, I will bring health and healing to it; I will heal my people and will let them enjoy abundant peace and security. (Jeremiah 33:6 NIV)

In 2011 and 2012, I worked independently as a contract psychologist throughout metro Atlanta. I loved the freedom that contract work offered, which allowed me to spend time with my young daughters and continue to work to complete my degree. But my spirit was unsettled. I was in a constant state of anxiety and panic over finances. You see, although contract work can be lucrative, I was still at the mercy of someone else deciding when I would be compensated for my work. At one point, I had been working three months and had not received one dime. The panic was so intense I could feel it in my body. I carried the unrest in my soul everywhere I went. There wasn't enough money to go around. We needed to pay the mortgage and buy diapers and food. You get the picture. I was angry. I had been working my butt off for three months and had yet to be paid. I felt unworthy, abused, and unappreciated.

The Law of Abundance is the simple fact that there is an unlimited Source of everything we need or could ever want. This great abundance is already ours, infinitely available to all of us, all the time. A key feature to this law is understanding that abundance has no limits. Although most people associate this law with financial prosperity, it extends to an abundance of everything this world has to offer: love, peace, joy, happiness, and more. Imagine that; there's no competition for anything in this world, none. The sun is the most appropriate representation to demonstrate the law of abundance. The sun is forever there, just shining on us. We had to do nothing to earn this; it simply does. So what did I do to activate abundance already there in my life?

My first step was understanding that it's God's plan for me to live an abundant life. Once I understood this, I just let go. I let go of trying to control my situation. I let go of allowing the stress of money to dictate my days, and I let go of the lie that there wasn't enough to go around because the Truth says there is! God wants to supply all your wants and needs, but He also wants you to have abundance for two other reasons. One, so you will share your overflow with others, and two, so others will see that He takes care of His people. And doesn't He say He'll do it?

When I got to this point, when I walked in the revelation of what this universal law says, peace, joy, and happiness overcame me. I wasn't worried about when or how things would happen. I settled in the knowing that I was being taken care of, I had more than enough, and what was mine was mine. Isn't that such a freeing way of life? And within a week, I kid you not, my money was there, just in time for my oldest daughter's birthday.

The Law of Action

Anyone who listens to the word but does not do what it says is like someone who looks at his face in a mirror and, after looking at himself, goes away and immediately forgets what he looks like. But whoever looks intently into the perfect law that gives freedom, and continue in it- not forgetting what they heard, but doing it- they will be blessed in what they do. (James 1:23-25 NIV)

For years I was so envious of my husband for the great friendships he had. He's had a very big and tight group of friends since junior high. The connection they have is unlike anything I've ever seen in my life. I've come to know these men as my brothers, and their constant support of me and my family is nothing short of a blessing. But they go on *way* too many trips together. Don't get me wrong. I love them and all, but I was really starting to hate on them for all the traveling they do together. And I would complain to Wesley that I didn't have friends to do those things with. He would say to me, "Then do it!" (Men are so simple, aren't they?). After an eye roll, and sucking my teeth, I would try to reason with him that it wasn't that easy. All my friends have young children, like I do. Scheduling and planning are just too difficult.

But really, it wasn't. I just needed to do it and so I did. I started calling up girlfriends and planning "girl's night" outings. Connection and sharing space with other women is a huge part of my spiritual makeup, and so I decided that I needed to feed my spirit and just do it. I took my husband's advice.

The Law of Action says that you can be the most gifted, intelligent, creative, honest, loving individual, but if you do not take action in your life, nothing will ever materialize. The Law of Action requires that you become a co-creator in your own life and that you no longer sit on the sidelines and watch it all go down. I love this law because, although we're talking about spiritual things here, it also takes some action to set that spiritual energy into motion. You are the leading actor and director of your own life, so get up and start to take some action to create what you want. The Universe will acknowledge your efforts and bless you along the way.

The Law of Expectation

Yes, my soul, find rest in God; my hope comes from him. (Psalms 62:5 NIV)

I made the hefty commute into Atlanta every day for

about two and a half years. In the event that you've never had the pleasure of dealing with Atlanta traffic, let me assure you that it's a blessing. It would take me anywhere from an hour and a half to two hours to get to my destination, and of course, no commute was the same. On any given day, I could even get lucky and manage to get there in an hour.

Either way, the commute put me in an emotional rollercoaster. But I expected that. I expected to be miserable and frustrated in the car, so you guessed it, that's exactly what happened. One day, I thought to myself, "This has got to get better. How can I make this situation better for me? I want to get to my destination refreshed, happy, and peaceful. What can I do to feel that way?"

I expected a different outcome, and I was going to do everything in my power to make sure this was the case. And that was when, one day at my local library, I stumbled upon audio books. I picked up a couple of self-help, positive, uplifting books to listen to on my commute, and what a difference they made in my life. I'm telling you that when you make a decision in your life, in this case my expectation to have a better commute, the Universe obliges and sends things your way to support you. The innocent introduction of audio books was my saving grace.

The Law of Expectation tells us that whatever we expect with confidence will become a self-fulfilling prophecy. In that instance, I decided I was going to be refreshed, happy, and peaceful. The Universe got in line with that decision and supported me along the way. Always expect the best, and this goes for the people around you as well. You could start in your own home by expecting the best from your spouse and children and backing up that expectation with positive words. Expect the best from yourself. You have an unlimited potential. You have to believe that and imagine yourself already where you want to be. There's nothing wrong with setting high expectations for yourself and for those around you. When you do so in a loving and supportive way, your loved ones will rise to the occasion.

The Law of Resistance

"Then why does God still blame us? For who is able to resist his will?"(Romans 9:19 NIV)

When we focus on a particular thing, we are in essence calling it into our lives, whether we want it or not. The Law of Resistance can be tricky because we often activate it unconsciously. You can call situations, people, or experiences you don't necessarily want into your life. Because you focused on it, it's there. This comes from a victim mentality, resisting generosity and abundance, and not taking personal responsibility for creating your situation. So how can you counteract the Law of Resistance?

I can't think of a better way to illustrate this law in action than through marriage. Once my husband and I started sharing a space together after we got married, I realized that he doesn't handle things the way I do. Cabinet doors were left open, lights left on, and empty boxes and old receipts piled up in random places. I would walk into the house and want to jump out of my skin because the space was so chaotic. I found myself in conversations with people saying things like, "He's so messy. I have to clean up after him." Oh, this is when you know you're really annoyed.

I'd be driving down the road, happy as can be, and all of a sudden, a flash of my messy kitchen would send me into a tailspin of anger, bitterness, and resentment. Whoa, problem! This was controlling my life, and worse yet, by the time I walked in the door, I was mad at my husband, and he didn't even know why. So of course, I had to let him know, and I went down my laundry list of how he was failing to pull his weight in the house. This was the wrong way to handle it. I was creating an enemy in my own house.

To trick the Law of Resistance, you must resist the negative and instead embrace the positive. What do I mean by that? I stopped using all my energy to focus on his faults and instead embraced all the great things he does. In this case, resisting just meant that I didn't give the negative any more of my energy. My energy was best focused on the positive because what you focus on grows.

So every time I felt myself going down the black hole of all the things he *didn't* do, I focused on all the great things he *did* do. And you know what? He started to do more good things in the house. Now is my house free of clutter? Of course not, and it never will be. That's just a fact of life. But now I'm not letting that have any power over me.

Activating the Law of Attraction Using Visualization

I love music. I love what music does to my soul. I love how the right song can take me right back to my years in high school, driving around in my Honda Prelude, or make me remember when I met my husband and fell in love. It's during those times, when I'm listening to music, that I can visualize things that I want to happen in my life. I have been visualizing for as long as I can remember, and I didn't even know it was a technique or skill. It was relaxing to me and my way of thinking about the future.

I spent the first eighteen years of my life in Indiana, and from the age of eight, I knew that I wouldn't spend the rest of my life there. I started sending interest letters to colleges in the fifth grade, asking them to send me their catalogs, and spent hours going through them, trying to determine which school I would go to. By the time I was sixteen, I spent evenings with my headphones on, listening to music, visualizing my departure from Indiana and my transition to college life. Over the last twenty years, I've visualized graduation, marriage, children, houses, and even this book here. And you know what? They have all come to pass.

Visualization is a conscious mental creation. When you use visualization to imagine things in your mind, you activate the Law of Attraction to make physical manifestations of those images come to reality. Visualizing the things you want to happen, as if they have already happened in your mind, is a way to trick your subconscious. You see, your subconscious is unable to distinguish between what is real and what is imagined. It will just react to the things you create in your mind as if they're real. Again, you have the power to co-create the life you've always wanted with the Universe by your side. What will you create?

CHAPTER SIX

Execute

Execute your plans with passion, love, and unwavering faith that they will be fruitful.

So you have all this information, strategies, and tips. Now what? Where do you go from here? I'm a believer that until you are able to walk in the revelation of the understanding of these concepts, that is, until you start to walk in the truth of what you believe, none of the information I've expressed in this book will be helpful to you. It's time to execute. It's time to stop sitting on the sidelines of life, get in the game, and play the game to win.

You've got an arsenal of information in this book to support your mind, body, and soul, but now you have to live this out *every day*. This has to become a priority in your life. You have to integrate the concepts found within these pages in every decision, experience, act, and thought of your life. But don't worry. I've got some more pointers to support you along the way.

Protect Your Mindset and Your Vision

I'll be completely honest with you, as I have throughout this entire book. On the journey of self-discovery, and in your life in general, attempting to better yourself and create the kind of life you desire, might cause people in your life to act a little funny. In my life, friendships have faded, new friendships have emerged, and I've chalked it all up to my continual and non-negotiable decision to put my personal evolution as a priority. As I continually evolved, I noticed that not everyone in my circle understood what I was doing or was happy that I was doing something. You may notice the same thing, but luckily for you, that's not your problem!

I've got stories for days to illustrate this concept, but I'll start with the one that first introduced me to it. As I explained to you in the last chapter, I knew I would not be living in Indiana once I graduated from high school, and I'd been dreaming of the day I'd leave since I was in elementary school. However, once I made the announcement to friends and family members that I was accepted to and would be attending Florida A&M University, in Tallahassee, Florida, many of them looked at me like I had three heads. I got comments like:

"Why would you go to school so far away?

"You don't know anyone there."

"Why would you want to go to a Black school?"

Looking back on it now, I can laugh, but at the time, I was very hurt and bothered by people's comments. I didn't understand why someone would want to purposefully devalue my decisions and my purpose. And then I realized something. They couldn't *see* my vision. They couldn't understand something that I had *known* for years.

For me, the pendulum swung all the way to the other side, and I didn't share any of my dreams with anyone because I was so afraid of someone crapping on them. It was killing me. Over the years, I found people along the way who I would confide in, but I have a very select few I trust with my deepest and most honest visions. Not everyone in your circle needs to be privy to your vision because, honestly, not everyone is happy that you're trying to become a better person.

Most people are comfortable with you right where you are, and if you move beyond that place, it can be confusing, frustrating, or discouraging to them. It can also remind them that they're not fully living out their own purpose. The trick here is to not focus on the negative parts of this concept, but to intentionally call into your life the people and situations that are going to be supportive of your evolution. As you intentionally do that, the right people will be drawn to you, and the wrong people will slowly start to drift away.

Pen and Paper Hold the Power

I've wanted to write a book for most of my life, and in fact, when I was young, I wanted to be a writer. Today, I can say that I am a writer and have *always* been a writer. But for years, as I thought about it, no concepts came to mind. I had no idea what I was going to write. I toyed with the idea of being a children's author for a while, but nothing ever materialized. Finally, in 2014, while on a solo trip to California, I pulled out my notebook and started to write down the skeleton of this book. At the time, I had no idea that this would be the end result, but this book was birthed on a plane with a pen and paper.

Life is so much simpler than we make it. As humans, we like to come up with all these complicated explanations for why things go wrong and why things don't happen, but when we really get down to the basics of life, it really is as simple as writing something down with pen and paper.

What do I mean by that? I'm talking about the power of writing down your goals, dreams, and aspirations. It's the power of putting something down in your own handwriting. It's your way of affirming what you want, and once again, the Universe acts accordingly. In fact, I'll take it a step further and tell you just how powerful and destiny-driven writing things down can be.

Right now, I have at least three notebooks around my house in which I write down ideas, goals, and anything that comes to my mind. I also have three journals, one of which stays in my purse at all times because my mind is always racing. As I started to write this chapter, I flipped back through my notebooks and journals, as I always do to look for ideas or anything to spark more inspiration, and I stumbled upon these concepts I've covered in this book. The date on that page was 10-10-14, exactly one year to the date of my book release, 10-10-15. I sat back in amazement and teared up, overcome with gratitude for that moment. Nothing could better illustrate the power of writing your goals down than this story. It still gives me chills just thinking about it.

You don't always need to have a purpose in mind when you put things down on paper. I didn't know the concepts I wrote down that day would turn into the chapters of this book you're reading one year later. On the flip side, if there is something you're specifically working toward or want to accomplish, put it down on paper. Even better, attach a date to it. Writing this book was a goal I wrote down with a completion date attached to it. Take it one step further, and tell one or two people in your trusted circle, people who will support you in protecting that goal and hold you accountable for making sure you achieve it.

The Power Is in the Ask

Speaking of your trusted circle, ask for help and support from people you trust and can count on to support you. I spoke about this strategy in chapter four, but it bears repeating, so here it is again. Asking can do several things for you. First, asking for what you want will help you gain more clarity. If you have to ask someone to support you in achieving a goal, you need to be able to explain to that person what the goal is, and how you would like them to support you. Next, asking is the action step in all that vision you have wrapped up in your head. So asking is your opportunity to get out of your head and start to receive. Remember that you're in the executing phase, so now you need to start *acting*. Last, asking breeds confidence. You may have a goal that you've been mulling over for months. You write it down on paper, but once you ask someone for help and articulate it aloud, it takes your goal-setting to another level. Closed mouths don't get fed, so ask away!

Straighten up Your Crown Queen, and Keep Steppin'

This is the simple acknowledgment and calling back into your present mind of the fact that you are a queen. You are unstoppable. You are royalty, and you are more powerful than you know. On the road to personal evolution and transformation, you will be knocked down, dragged through the mud, stepped on, talked about, and even mocked, but I encourage you to straighten up that crown, remember your birthright, and keep it moving! But how can you remind yourself of this fact every day? Here are some tips:

1.   Keep a gratitude journal or gratitude box. Getting in the habit of consistently writing down something *good* that happened every day, no matter how small, will keep your mindset focused on the positive, which will only bring more positive your way. In fact, our family keeps a gratitude box that stays in the family room of our house. We all drop notes about each other in the box throughout

the year, and on December 31st, we review the box together as a family. It's a great way to show gratitude and appreciation to each other. I'm in the process of starting one just for me, specific to my own unique journey.

2.   Spend fifteen to twenty minutes a day listening to or reading something motivational or uplifting. If you completed the exercises in the earlier chapter, you'll know your strengths and peak time of the day to accomplish things. If you're a morning person, you may try reading a few pages in the morning before work. As I wrote about, I started listening to audio books on my long commute. Now I listen to podcasts, interviews, and whatever I can get my hands on to keep me motivated.

3.   Surround yourself with visual representations of your new mindset, like quotes and sayings, or a vision board. Over the years, I've placed sticky notes with motivational sayings or goals on my mirror in the bathroom. I also make my own vision boards and follow people on social media who are positive and uplifting. My home also reflects my lifestyle. I choose artwork with

uplifting statements to bring positivity to our space.

Don't Tip the scales!

Too much of one thing is never good, so allow this to be your gentle reminder that your new lifestyle is all about balance. On the journey to personal transformation, you will have moments of extreme highs and lows. There will be time spent in the valley, spiritual breakthroughs, bouts of pain and fear, revelation, and silence that can threaten your stability. I urge you to balance the potentially bumpy ride with self-love practices. My favorite practices involve both rest and play.

I know it sounds simple, but there need to be moments in your life when you allow yourself to just be, no deadlines, no expectations, just be. Resting isn't always about sleeping, although I am a huge proponent of getting enough sleep and napping when your body feels the urge. The art of resting also includes the ability to let go and surrender parts of your life to God. You've heard lawyers say, "I rest my case, your Honor." Well, sometimes it's okay to rest certain situations in your life, especially when you've done your part. There's got to be this healthy give and take, a spiritual dance, between you and God. There are going to moments when you know it's your time to put your head down and grind it out, and other times when He says to you, "Good job. Now let me take it from here." The trick is to stay close to Him and obey those gentle nudges.

Another self-love practice to incorporate in your life is play. I have to thank Wesley for helping me to realize the importance of play. He loves to have fun! Play, for me, is an emotional release, a time to let loose and be wild and crazy. For my husband and me, the world is our playground, and we use travel to kick back and play. We are also avid concert attendees, our favorites being hip hop shows. When an artist we love hits the stage, Wesley and I are like little kids, singing and dancing along. We both have such an affinity for music, and the release we feel and connection we have to it creates more intimacy for our marriage.

But what about something more simple? We have pillow fights and chase each other around the house too. Play for adults may seem trivial and childish to some, but play brings joy and happiness when you're in that moment. Finally, play with kids. They remind us how simple life really is. I still play with my daughters. And if you're going to do it, go all in. I get completely into their world and allow them to take the lead.

In chapter two, we talked about acknowledging the things that aren't working in your life. This brutal honesty is necessary to bring forth the things that aren't working. The things I've described in this book actually do work, as positive, warm and fuzzy, or cheesy as they may sound. However, you must understand that the things I'm suggesting you do can't be done half-ass. You can't be on the fence about this kind of work. That's exactly why so many of the things I've poured out in this book can be interpreted as silly or "woo woo." People try them half-heartedly, and then get mad when they don't work.

You can't truly activate any of the amazingly powerful benefits of these practices without *intention*. Dr. Wayne Dyer, one of my favorite personal development experts, said, "Guidance is always available when you are open to it, and when you are aligned in body, mind, and spirit." When your mind (thoughts) is in alignment with your body (actions), and you have a *purpose* for using the practices, you will experience miraculous transformation in your life.

I've given you everything I know to help you embark on your own personal journey of transformation. This has been an amazing experience to pour my knowledge, experience, and life onto the pages of this book with you. Sharing my story has allowed me to realize just how powerful I am, and in turn, I want to see you strong and powerful as well. So be brave, be scared, be happy, be sad, be angry, be elated, be courageous, be vulnerable in your life, in your relationships, and most importantly, with yourself.

You deserve everything this world has to offer. I promise you that. You just have to *believe* it, *act* upon that knowing, and call on God and His infinite Universe to help you make it happen. My journey is by no means over, my friend, and as I learn and experience more in life, I will *always* come back and share it with you.

REFERENCES

Dweck, C.S. (2007). Mindset: The new psychology of success. New York: Random House.

Lally, P., Wardle, J., & Gardner, B. (2011). Experiences of habit formation: A qualitative study. *Psychology, Health & Medicine. 16, 484–489.* doi:10.1080/13548506.2011.555774.

Lovitts, B. (2001). Leaving the ivory tower: The causes and consequences of departure from doctoral study (New York: Rowman & Littlefield Publishers, 2001).

Mahoney, S. (2009). Mindset change influences on student buy-in to online classes. *Quarterly Review of Distance Education, 10*(1), 75-83, 90. Retrieved from http://search.proquest.com/docview/231183227?accountid=134574.

Rogers, E. M. (1995). *Diffusion of innovations* (4th ed.). New York: The Free Press.

US Department of Education, National Center for Education Statistics (USDE, NCES), "Condition of Education 2010," http://nces.ed.gov/fastfacts/display.asp?id=72 (accessed Jul 2, 2015).

Williamson, M. (1992). *A return to love reflections on the principles of a course on miracles.* New York: Harper Collins.

Zacks, J. M., Speer, N. K., Swallow, K. M., Braver, T. S., & Reynolds, J. R. (2007). Event perception: A mind-brain perspective. *Psychological Bulletin, 133, 273–293.* doi:10.1037/0033-2909.133.2.273.

Before You Go…

Did you download my FREE Become You Resource

Companion? Head over to www.tonekaetienne.com to get

your additional resources.

CPSIA information can be obtained at www.ICGtesting.com
Printed in the USA
BVOW05s2207161215

430494BV00005B/551/P